Yellowstone National Park

A Natural Wonder

By Marla Tomlinson

Discover Plants and Animals
Vowel Teams Review

Scan this code to access the Teacher's Notes for this series or visit
www.norwoodhousepress.com/decodables

NORWOOD HOUSE  PRESS

DEAR CAREGIVER, *The Decodables* series contains books following a systematic, cumulative phonics scope and sequence aligned with the science of reading. Each book allows its reader to apply their phonics knowledge in engaging and relatable texts. The words within each text have been carefully selected to ensure that readers can rely on their decoding skills as they encounter new or unfamiliar words. They also include high frequency words appropriate for the target skill level of the reader.

When reading these books with your child, encourage them to sound out words that are unfamiliar by attending to the target letter(s) and sounds. If the unknown word is an irregularly spelled high frequency word or a word containing a pattern that has yet to be taught (challenge words) you may encourage your child to attend to the known parts of the word and provide the pronunciation of the unknown part(s). Rereading the texts multiple times will allow your child the opportunity to build their reading fluency, a skill necessary for proficient comprehension.

You can be confident you are providing your child with opportunities to build their decoding abilities which will encourage their independence as they become lifelong readers.

Happy Reading!

Emily Nudds, M.S. Ed Literacy
Literacy Consultant

Norwood House Press • www.norwoodhousepress.com
The Decodables ©2024 by Norwood House Press. All Rights Reserved.
Printed in the United States of America.
367N–082023

Library of Congress Cataloging-in-Publication Data has been filed and is available at
https://lccn.loc.gov/2023012390

Literacy Consultant: Emily Nudds, M.S.Ed Literacy
Editorial and Production Development and Management: Focus Strategic Communications Inc.
Editors: Christine Gaba, Christi Davis-Martell
Photo Credits: Shutterstock: AJ13 (p. 6), Cavan-Images (p. 21), COLBY MARTZALL (p. 19), crbellette (p. 12), Dmitry Kovba (p. 9), Don Mammoser (cover, pp. 4–5), Erinn Hermsen (p. 9), Harold Collins Photography (p. 14), jack-sooksan (p. 20), Jemini Joseph (p. 17), Jnjphotos (p. 10), Ken Ringer (p. 15), Kevin Wells Photography (p. 15), Lane V. Erickson (p. 21), Lu Yang (p. 9), Macrovector (covers), melissamn (p. 8), Michael Benard (p. 19), Michael Tatman (p. 11), MisterStock (p. 11), M. Leonard Photography (p. 16), Oliver S (p. 9), Rainer Lesniewski (p. 7), Susanne Pommer (p. 9), Teresa Otto (p. 13), Wellford Tiller (p. 10), Wirestock Creators (p. 16), Yizhuo (p. 18).

Hardcover ISBN: 978-1-68450-683-5   Paperback ISBN: 978-1-68404-907-3
eBook ISBN: 978-1-68404-962-2

Contents

Yellowstone National Park

It's Monday at Yellowstone National Park. The cars on the road just **creep** along. It is so slow. But it is not a **traffic jam**. You are in a bison jam!

A slow pack of these big animals is on the road.

This is a sight you can see a lot in Yellowstone. It is where the largest **herd** of wild bison in North America roam. It can be a long wait for them to leave.

Bison that roam on the road can be in the way of drivers.

Yellowstone is home to many animal **species** and habitats. This is due to its size and where it is. It is over two million acres.

A place this big has a lot of food and water for animals. There are many trees and plants that make seeds and nuts for a meal.

You can meet a goat in the mountain. A crow may fly in the valley. A goose might take a swim in the creek. Or a bee may enjoy a flower bloom in the field.

There are so many habitats in the park.

Yellowstone has many different areas for animals to live, like this canyon.

The main part of the park is in Wyoming. Parts of the park reach into Montana and Idaho.

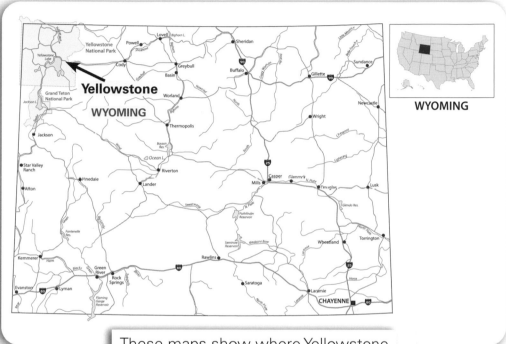

WYOMING

These maps show where Yellowstone Park can be found.

FUN FACT

Yellowstone was the first national park in the world! It was founded in 1872.

Heat in the Ground

Yellowstone is on top of the world's largest active volcano. Its last blow was over 70,000 years ago.

This gives the area **hydrothermal** features. These are areas where there is a lot of heat. It makes the water very hot.

You can see steam raise up from the land and water.

It may seem like these areas with high heat may be right for animals. But it is too hot! They may die if they try to drink this water. You will not see animals in this part of the park.

This geyser is called Old Faithful because it blows steam and water at regular times.

A geyser is a special hydrothermal feature. A geyser is a **vent** in the ground that gets so much heat that it blows steam and water out of the hole.

Types of Hydrothermal Features			
Steam vents		Geysers	
Mud pots		Hot springs	

You might not see animals, but there are living things in this high heat. There are very small **organisms** there that love the heat.

They are so small that you can't see each one, but you can see what looks like mats of color. These are the tiny organisms grouped together in **trillions**.

This lake has bands of different colors made by groups of tiny organisms.

Different species of organisms are different colors.

The Grand Prismatic Spring in Yellowstone is the biggest hot spring in the park. It has mats of bright color from the tiny things that live there. The heat of the water makes this the right habitat for them.

The water is between 145°F and 188°F. You can see the steam rise off the water!

The Grand Prismatic Spring boasts many colors and it is very hot.

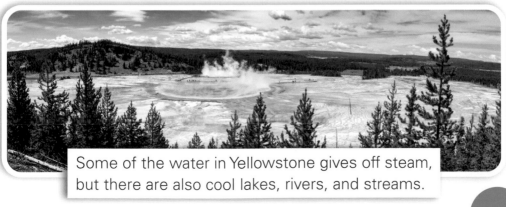

Some of the water in Yellowstone gives off steam, but there are also cool lakes, rivers, and streams.

Large Animals and the Food They Eat

You might meet an elk when you are out on a trail in the park. There are over 10,000 elk in the park in the summer. Many elk leave the park in the winter.

An elk is part of the deer family. Elk are big and have thick coats.

An elk looks for food in the snow at Yellowstone.

Quaking aspen trees are found in Yellowstone.

Elk live in forest habitats and feed on plants and trees.

Elk think aspen trees make a good meal. In the past, elk ate the **shoots** from the trees before they had a chance to grow. This almost made aspen trees die off. When more gray wolves came to the park, they hunted elk. This meant fewer elk chewed the young aspen. So now the Aspen tree grows again in the park.

13

Bighorn sheep can also be seen in Yellowstone. These sheep live in alpine habitats and grasslands. They migrate between the two.

They eat grass, plants, and weeds. Their hoof feet make it easy to get by on steep hills and cliffs.

A male bighorn sheep is called a ram. A ram's horns are about three feet across. The female sheep also has horns, but they are smaller.

Moose in Yellowstone can grow to almost seven feet tall. It is hard to know for sure how many moose there are in the park. They live deep in the woods. The trees make them hard to see.

This moose came out of the woods to look for food.

Do not stray far from the trail when on a hike. There are a lot of bears in the park. Keep safe and steer clear of both the black bear and the grizzly.

Bears need to eat a lot. They think trout found in lakes and streams are a treat. It is a key food they eat.

A large bighorn ram's horns can weigh almost 30 pounds!

These bighorn sheep rest on the mountain.

This grizzly found a fish in the stream.

Small Animals in the Park

Pikas are small animals that live in alpine areas. They do not like the heat so they stay where it is cool. They even like the snow. They look like rabbits with small ears. They get their **fuel** from grass and plants.

Pikas are gray or brown. This helps them blend in with the rocks.

The marten is a type of sleek weasel that you would meet in the park. They live in forests, meadows, and alpine regions. This makes Yellowstone a great place for them.

Pikas make a loud and high squeak when they speak.

Martens live in **hollow** trees, rock piles, or burrows.

There are many bats that fly around the park. But have no fear! They sleep in the day and go out at night.

The park has many other small animals that you may see around your house.

Squirrels can be seen as they play in the trees. Skunks roam the fields. Mice make their way in the grass. Raccoons come out at night to find some food.

FUN FACT

Some bats eat their body weight in bugs each night!

This skunk in Yellowstone National Park has a fluffy tail.

Water Is Life

The rain and snow help the water flow. There are over 1,000 rivers and streams in the park. There are 600 lakes. The water helps keep animals and plant life alive.

Yellowstone Lake is a cool lake. It does not have the heat of other water in the park. In fact, it will freeze over in winter.

Yellowstone Lake is the biggest lake in the park.

There are **native** fish in the park. Some fish are trout. The main kind of trout is the cutthroat trout. Many animals rely on this breed of fish for food. Because they feed so many animals, people are not able to keep them. If they catch a cutthroat trout or any native fish, they must put them back. This fish has a red line that helps show what kind of trout it is.

A cutthroat is released in the water.

The western toad lives in or near water. They eat bees, ants, and other bugs. They spend their day below logs and rocks, or in the water.

The western toad is green and gray with a white stripe down its back.

Open For All to See

Yellowstone National Park is seen by over four million people a year. They enjoy the sights of animals and plants. They also see the hot water areas.

People should stay back from the animals and not feed them. And they should stay on the trail around the hot water and steam.

People walk on a boardwalk to see the steam rise from the ground.

If you want to bring your boat, you need to clean it well and drain any water in it first. This keeps the fish and plant life in Yellowstone safe from anything not native to the area.

If you follow the park rules, you will stay safe and be free to enjoy your time at the park. You will see and hear many amazing things.

You must stay back from the geysers at the park.

A person fishes on vacation while a bison stands nearby.

Glossary

creep: move slowly

fuel: gives energy, like food or gas

herd: large group of animals

hollow: empty

hydrothermal (hī-drō-thər-mŭl): hydro means water and thermal means hot; hot water

native (nā-tŭv): from that area

organisms (ōr-gŭn-ĭz-ŭmz): very tiny living things

shoots: young trees

species (spē-sēz): group of animals that are the same type

traffic jam: so many cars they can't go fast or go at all

trillions (TRIL-yunz): thousands of billions (a very big number!)

vent: an open spot that lets things out, like steam

Index

Vowel Teams

ea/ee/ey			oa/oe/ow		ai/ay		ie/igh
bee	hear	seen	below	grow	day	raise	bright
breed	heat	sheep	blow	hollow	drain	stay	die
clean	keep	sleek	boardwalk	know	gray	stray	high
clear	key	speak	boasts	road	main	tail	might
creek	leave	squeak	boat	roam	may	trail	night
creep	meal	steam	coats	show	play	wait	right
deep	meet	steer	crow	slow	rain	way	sight
deer	near	stream	flow	snow			
fear	need	three	follow	toad			
feed	reach	tree	goat				
feet	see	weeds					
free	seeds	year					
freeze	seem						

oo/ue			Vowel y		Vowel teams in two syllable words	
bloom	food	hoof	by	try	Monday	released
cool	fuel	moose	fly		raccoons	valley
due	goose	shoots				

High-Frequency Words

again	before	found	large	over	very
also	different	great	live	should	want
animal	does	kind	old	small	world
because	even	know			

Challenging Words

area(s)	feature	hydrothermal	native	weight
bear	geyser	Idaho	organisms	Wyoming
bison	ground			